1: The value of money.

- Mr. Danglar. Can you tell me what the money is?

- Of course, my dear Eduardo. Money is a convention, an agreement between individuals who belong to a society, that gives symbolic value to a set of currencies, generally legal, to facilitate the exchange of goods and services.

- Does this mean that money is not necessarily issued in central banks?

- Rather, it means that a society can use anything as money. However, this 'thing' should have value in itself; this is the case of precious metals such as silver and gold. Its importance comes from the fact that each one is a limited good, very useful in itself and since everyone is interested in it, that is, they demand it, they keep their value high.

- But.... why does the value of gold rise? A kilogram of gold still weighs the same today as when the grandfather was a child, but according to the account, its cost always soars upwards.

- Ah! Eduardo, what happens is that goods change in value over time, since their demand (people who need them) and the level of supply (people who want to sell) are also dynamic, they change over time. Demand, for example, is multifactorial and often only one of these factors is enough to increase the price of goods; I know, for example, that when you play sports and are thirsty, you would easily dare to pay three times the value of a bottle of water; well, I assure you that if the young man who serves in the coffee shop knew it, he would charge you for it. I also know that if there is only one bottle of water available and all your friends would like to buy it, you will pay more than triple its value. Something similar happens with gold and other goods. If the number of people interested in a kilogram of gold is much higher than the number of kilograms of gold available for sale in the same period of time, the value of gold will increase, while if it is much lower, it will decrease in price, as is the case with the prices of tomatoes, mangoes, lemons or avocados on the market.

- It's true," said Eduardo looking at Mr. Danglar with excitement, "I remember that at the beginning and end of the mango season, mangoes cost twice as much as their usual price, compared to when there are many mangoes.

- And also Eduardo, that's why they sell the dozens cheaper or as we say in the market, better the wholesale price than the retail.

- Um...'Cheaper by the dozen', I understand, is because there are more.

- The correct term to explain that, from a money perspective, my dear Eduardo, is inflation and deflation with respect to the start of the mango season, when a kilogram of gold can buy up to 100 mangoes. Let's see: a deflation in the currency, allows that, with the same amount of gold with which at the beginning of the season you could only buy 100 mangos, you can then acquire more than 100; if on the contrary, the currency is affected by inflation, then you will need more than one kilogram of gold, to be able to buy 100 mangos. This explains the rise and fall in the prices of a wide variety of goods.

- Money is a very complicated thing, Mr. Danglar. But I see it's so important, I'd like to know more. Another question, and excuse me Mr. Danglar, can you tell me why some people have so much money and others have so little?

- Well my dear Eduardo, there are so many reasons that I don't know where to start; perhaps one of the most influential reasons is the indiscipline of spending, which together with the ignorance of the value of money, exposes young people like you to the risk of capital flight. Many people are poor and always lack money because they do not learn to spend correctly the little money they have.

- It is said that people who don't go to school are ignorant, isn't it? However, my grandfather knows many people who became rich and never finished school.

- We are all ignorant my dear Eduardo, but not all of us are ignorant of the same things. Ignoring is almost synonymous with unknown and although there are people who ignore the appropriate terms or words, they have well established concepts that allow them to refer to these words, that is, they know the meaning of these words, even without knowing the exactly name by which they are called for in economic experts; therefore they are not completely ignorant and without going to school, they can become rich because they have learned in the streets the meaning of correct use of money. That is to say, those people you mention have learned through experience not to spend their available resources on anything they don t need, and they jealously guard some money in order to take advantage of the opportunities that arise or deal with the emergencies that may come up in their lives. But Eduardo, this is not the easiest way to learn, it is not the most effective way either; you will see how finishing school gives you many advantages in all your ways, because studying will allow you to have a lot of useful and important information, which you can use to improve your life and entrepreneurship in the area of business and finance.

- But how can some people know something so difficult without going to school? I don't get it.

- Nothing could be easier. With the help of intelligence and of course using the scientific method, even if they do not know the name. I also believe that a little luck puts them on the right track and their minds and intelligence helps them to learn from the small experiences they have had.

- I want to understand it, especially if you're sure that learning it can help me get rich.

- Of course, Eduardo. I'm sure you've practiced it many times, I also know that it's an information that will be given to you at school, although sadly I don't think you'll be informed that it also helps people to produce wealth. Teachers appear to ignore it or have such confidence in kids as young as your age that they think they will learn it on their own.

- No, I've never used that method. And if I did, I think I would be rich already, because after I learn it I know I would never stop practicing it.

- It's just that it's not that easy, there are more things people have to learn in order to get rich. But let's see whether or not you used the scientific method first, and then I'll tell you. Okay?

- All right - exclaimed Eduardo with a defiant attitude - you will see that I have never used it, if I were, I would know it if I were intelligent.

- Have you observed any phenomenon or activity? Yes. Have you made any inductions about that phenomenon or activity? Yes. Have you hypothesized about that which you have observed? Yes, have you experimented with that activity or phenomenon? Of course you have and I am sure you have demonstrated or discarded them. Well, Eduardo, when these steps are properly applied to the same activity sequentially, they constitute the scientific method, and if you apply it properly, you can achieve great results and learn a number of wonderful things about any activity. Think back to when schools didn't exist, how do you think people learned things then?

- I never thought about that before, but I guess someone was showing them to him.

- Gee," said Mr. Danglar excitedly, "that's a really good answer, but what about the people who learned them first, no one could teach them, so?

Schools serve to teach a group of people at the same time, with the intention that society should transmit to future generations a basic knowledge that will facilitate learning and understanding later on, any branch of all collective knowledge that has accumulated thanks to the contributions of men and women of the past and that we have preserved through books. Individuals were destined to learn by themselves the things that seemed interesting to them; a general knowledge base had to be guaranteed, which would make it easier for the younger ones to assimilate the previous knowledge, but there were so many things to learn or be interested in that it was impossible to determine what would be necessary and what would not be necessary to fix the knowledge of the things that were interesting to children after they became adults.

In the face of this situation and with humanity having many books available, it was decided to teach how to read to little ones, because no matter in what they are most interested in tomorrow, reading is how they are going to find it in books, to learn.

It was then necessary to develop the lesson plans for schools, and to include all the useful information that is generally used in all disciplines, regardless of the subject matter or branch of knowledge. That's why we are all taught colors, counting, adding, multiplying, geometric shapes, reading, writing and so on. In this way society helps us and prepares us to quickly learn the things we think are interesting, without having to spend as much time as the time spent by the human being who first learned them, and better still, without having to make the same mistakes.

Mr. Danglar explained all this to our Eduardo as they continued to argue.

- But Mr. Danglar, there's something I don't understand, you say I've used the scientific method, but I don't remember ever using it, no activity I've done sequentially comes to my mind, and I don't quite understand what it means by the same phenomenon.

- I'll help you jog your memory, dear boy. When you watch the baseball games (observation) you figure the trajectory of the ball (induction). Depending on the speed, the strength of the ballplayer and the direction in which the ball is going, you imagine that the strong strokes will take it further than the weak strokes (Hypothesis) and when you play yourself, then you experience and draw your own conclusion; this is how you use the scientific method, because you're learning comes from experience.

- Well, I do use the scientific method. I never knew, but I do.

- Dear Eduardo, what do you think is necessary to know and do to become a rich man or woman?

- I don't know, Mr. Danglar, but I want to know. I want to be rich. I really want it.

- Do you know what it means to be rich, young Edward?

- Of course, having a lot of money. That's what it's all about.

- And how much is a lot?

- Millions, many millions.

- Do you know Eduardo that you can be a millionaire and not feel like you're a rich man?

- How is that possible? If I had a lot of money, if I had millions, I would already be rich and it would not be possible for me not to feel that way.

- What do you want them for, Eduardo? What do you want with so many millions? Will they help you buy happiness?

- Yes! If I could have the things I want, that would make me happy. When I'm a millionaire I'll be rich and I'll have happiness.

- I don't doubt it, my dear Eduardo, you'd feel happy. But maybe now you're rich, too, and you ignore it.

- A person who doesn't have money can't be rich," said Eduardo bragging about his intelligence'', so I'm not a rich person.

- That's where you're wrong, dear Eduardo. You're confused. I invite you to make use of your prodigious mind and reflect. I tell you that there are very rich people with little money and there are poor people, without real wealth, but whose bank accounts handle a few million a year. This is so because poverty is in the mind, but wealth is also in the mind. Being rich is something you have to learn how to be, just like being an electrician, doctor or plumber; being rich is a trade.

- Please, Mr. Danglar! - The young man exclaimed, "Don't make fun of me, I love you very much and I have a lot of respect for you, please don't make fun of me.

- I'm not making fun of my boy. I'm going to help you out of this mess, I promise. But I'd like to know if you know something important, something that every rich person knows.

- What is it? Ask me to see.

- Dear Eduardo, how much do you cost?

" all the gold in the world " said the boy without mistake. However, this question was asked by Mr. Danglar without referring to a sale. The question had a more elegant, sophisticated and particular interest. Rather than ask him, he wanted to tell the boy that everything has an associated cost, whose value increases or decreases according to the circumstances, the individual, his environment, and his aspirations and very significantly according to his possibilities.

2: How much do you cost?

Every day, you are consuming scarce resources all the time, that is, resources that have value and that if it weren't for the limits naturally imposed by the circumstances in which you live, you would consume many more. Therefore, it is important to know, how much it costs to ensure the supply of the resources you need to consume so that you do not run out completely before the end of each month.

- When I ask how much do you cost Eduardo, what I want you to tell me is what resources you need to live with the level of comfort you currently have.

- You mean the amount of money I consume?

- Not my dear boy. It is true that it can be represented with a monetary value, but you know that this will vary greatly depending on inflation or deflation. If you do the experiment, you will see that every three or six months that monetary value will vary, but it is very likely that the real cost, your real cost, will remain the same for all that time.

- Then explain to me what you mean. I don't quite understand you. I have an idea, but I don't know if that's what you want to know.

- Well, go on, dare. You have nothing to lose if you answer whatever you think. If you are right, I will be very happy to see that your mind is as privileged as I imagine it to be, otherwise, I will give you the gift of knowledge. You have nothing to lose by trying something that costs you little or nothing. You are part of the sector of people who can be called young and as such must be bold, determined, cautious but launched. I'm sure you've heard the phrase "who doesn't take risks never wins" before.

- You're right, Mr. Danglar, I'll answer you then. As I understand it, a resource is everything that is consumed or spent; rather, all that can be used is a resource. That being so, food, water, notebooks and money are the resources you ask me about.

- Excellent, very good!

Mr. Danglar applauded little Eduardo and that clear way of explaining what a resource is. Be proud to have the friendship of such an intelligent young man.

- Tell me Eduardo then, what are all the resources you spend every month?

- Let's see - said the boy with a smile on his lips - food, water, notebooks, pencil, candy,...

- That's all very well," Danglar interrupted, "you pay for all that, but there's much more to it and you need to delete some things from that list, as long as we value more appropriately how much you cost. Let's order it now in the order of importance and choose only the things that are essential for you to live worthily every month, so we know what you cost, how much you cost and what you must do to become a rich man.

- I'm fine with it, Mr. Danglar. The most important thing is the food.

- Of course. Food is the first and most important resource for living in dignity; then we can include the house.

- Oh the house! - said the boy in surprise.

- Of course, the house is a very expensive resource, as much or more than food for most people. It is one of the most appreciated and important resources, even fundamental to a child's dignity.

- But the house doesn't cost me anything, it's my parents who take care of these things.

- But it won't be like that forever, nor will it be like that for all children. Did you know that some people live on the streets, that they have no protection from the weather, that they have no fixed place to eat or sleep, but that they are adrift, moving by God's mercy from one place to another without knowing where it is best?

- Yes, I have seen some young people my own age in such situations and it makes me very sad. I wish I could help them.

- That's all very well, but you should know how much you cost before you reach out to help others. It is necessary that you learn to give without being affected, to collaborate always when you can, so that you give with happiness and joy, so that you do not suffer or suffer any remorse. It's wonderful to give to those who need it, but it's much better if you give and don't need that thing you give away. Some have said, "Whoever gives what he possesses will beg for it. It is not true, the correct phrase would be ʺ who gives what he does not have to give, is going to beg and lament ʺ.

- But if you give something it's because it's yours, or at least you have it, isn't it, Mr. Danglar?

- Sometimes Eduardo, we give what we don't have or spend it badly. That is, giving or spending our available resources, regardless of how much we would need them for ourselves later on. Doing so puts us in trouble, limits our comfort and, as a consequence, sometimes pushes us to acquire harmful debts, from which we cannot easily get rid of, because ignorantly, we choose to go to a possible precipice, then we are trapped, imprisoned by our mistakes, with a flight of resources that we cannot cover up without help, thus keeping our lives in poverty.

- Well, it is important to know how much a person costs, and apparently it is also important to identify what resources are available. I see that if we give what we don't have to share, then we will need it and it would be like doing evil to ourselves.

- That's right, Eduardo, pay attention, I'll tell you right away how much you cost. You cost the resources that are indispensable for you to exist in the society, with the level of comfort that you now enjoy. In the case of an employee or worker like your mother or father, it would cost the resources that are indispensable for them to maintain their level of comfort, just like you, but also allow them to produce or supply the resources that meet their needs every month. For example, in the case of your father, he costs the food he needs to eat every month to be strong and healthy, he costs the clothes he needs to go to work every day of the month, he costs the number of bottles of water he consumes every day during the month, he also costs the value of the rent of the house, he costs the value of the gas the car consumes to get to and from work, he also costs the minimum resources he supplies you with and for whom if he doesn't do so the justice would take away his freedom. What he doesn't cost are the resources that are consumed on field trips for fun, the consumption of candy, the expenses on cable and technology that don't help them stay alive, or help them produce other resources and are not useful to solve a need, but create them.

- waoj now I understand, '' I cost '' is like saying: these are my needs, these are the resources I would not live without, without which I could not generate the resources I need every month and day by day.

- That's right, my dear Eduardo. Knowing this, can you guess what makes a person rich?

The boy looked at him thoughtfully without knowing what to say, but he was very excited. He felt great satisfaction because his mind would learn something new. Many questions and answers crossed his mind like lightning, he was looking for an answer to offer; he was really excited, he was very happy to be able to count on his friend Mr. Danglar.

- I understand from the question that it is not about money, that is to say that it is not specifically about resources, Mr. Danglar. One day I heard a phrase I remember at this moment, " the richest is not the one who has more, but the one who needs less ".

- Very brave," exclaimed Danglar". What makes a person rich, my dear Eduardo, is that he does not need or lack the resources that are essential for him to live with dignity, something that even if he does not work, he can maintain his level of comfort.

- That's why you said before, that maybe I'm rich even if I ignore it.

- Exactly. You, by the way, in my opinion are very rich, according to the representation of wealth that we have just made. But I want to show you a broader and more wonderful perspective of wealth, I want you to know the financial freedom with which people are really and wonderfully rich.

- woo, financial freedom. That sounds like fantasy and magical dreaming; it sounds like winning the lottery.

- Many people who won the lottery could not become wealthy because they did not achieve financial freedom. I want you to pay close attention to what I am going to tell you Eduardo, write it down in your mind and heart and teach it to your friends and children when you have them.

Mr. Danglar continued to instruct the boy, to open his mind, to introduce him to a world of ideas that he and no other young man in his school had ever encountered before.

Theme 3: financial freedom.

One of the best things in life, without a doubt, is freedom, we like it and it draws our attention powerfully. We have been tempted by this idea since adolescence. Everyone inside wants to be free, to have the opportunity to do what they want, when they want and how they want, no matter what. Many of us feel a little hope as we approach legal age, we know that there is a longed-for freedom that we can fulfill, but as time goes by we realize that things do not happen as in our dreams and that there is always a cost to pay for being free.

At 14 you are allowed to watch a new variety of TV shows, but you have to avoid having your little brother (or sister) watch them, because it is your responsibility, he or she is sitting next to you watching the TV and you cannot take him or her out of the room where the TV is located, just because you want him or her to be away. At the age of 14, you are allowed to go to bed an hour and a half later, but at 9 p.m., even if you are awake, you cannot be outside the house; you can have a cell phone, but you can't assign passwords to it, you can go out alone to visit some friends at their homes without the company of an adult, as long as your friend's parents are at home and call to let your parents know when you arrive and when you leave; at 14, you can also go to the workshop to learn a trade, but without any payment.

When you reach the age of 16, if you have your parents' permission you can work and that is when you have the experience of producing your own money. However, your lack of knowledge does not allow you to make good use of the capital that you have just deposited into your personal accounts. You are surprised, you get excited and you think that it is a lot, that you can buy with that amount all you want, then you learn that it is not enough (because the needs are dynamic and many of these are given by the income level). Your mother tells you that you must collaborate with something at home, your father tells you that you must give something to your mother, your desire to enjoy your money grows in you, you want to go for a walk to your grandmother's house with your friends, you want to go to the park, you want to do a lot of fun things and then you realize that you don't have enough money, so you learn again that you are not free to do what you want.

- Eduardo, before we talk about financial freedom, let's talk about financial slavery, I want to know what ideas you have about debts, tell me how do you think are originated and how do you think they can be eliminated. I want to know what you think about it, kid.

- Well, Mr. Danglar. Financial slavery is debt. I know because I've seen people in serious trouble for them, my Aunt Luisa is an example. I believe that debts are the resources you have committed to pay off for the next month without the month yet having started. They originate because people take loans. And how are they eliminated? Well, I think or rather I'm sure they're eliminated by paying for them.

- Well, that's an excellent answer, Eduardo. Although I would say that financial slavery is the lack of time and resources to do whatever you want. Debts, as you said before, are the situation that forces you to use your available resources to assign them to someone else, plus some interest. Interest will always be added to the money borrowed. This happens because before granting the loan, the person who gave it, whoever it was, considered that as payment for the money that has been lent, it needs to collect interest, which makes the debts bad. Of course, not all debts are necessarily bad, because there are debts that can help you build wealth.

- But what's this about interest? Why don't I just pay back what I borrowed?

- Well, it's very easy, remember I told you that people can't give what they don't have? So a lender is an individual or an institution that knows this perfectly well and when it lends something, it has to receive what it lent and also additional resources to those it originally lent. This is how they justify lending their resources to others, who they have obtained with great effort, at the risk of not being paid. That additional resource is what is known as interest, which is also the payment that creditors receive for lending their money to someone.

- Wow! They get paid without working, I want to be a loan shark. Said the boy with determination, 'That's what I want. I'm sure it'll make me a millionaire. If I get what I lent and I also get free resources, I will become very rich.

- Yes, maybe you can, but aren't you forgetting something very important?

- What's that?

- well, that the resources you want to lend can't be needed. Well, imagine they won't pay you back the resources borrowed, or the interest. You'll lose money and no one gets rich that way. Do you realize?

- ...it's true. It's true! It's true! - Said Eduardo with his hands on his head - and how am I going to get the resources I can afford?

- Let's think again, Eduardo, and don't worry, I'll tell you. Look, you know how much you cost and you know what your available resources are, that is, what you produce or what you own; so, it is easy to know now how many resources you have left to use freely, because reserving the resources that you cost will substantially reduce the risk of spending everything on entertainment and if you had a project that needs resources, you can now save them. Another thing you can do is to optimize your monthly cost. By efficiently using the resources you have available and making every effort over the course of a season to increase your savings capacity, you can more quickly put together the resources you want to start a project with.

- Excuse me, Mr. Danglar, when you talk about saving, do you mean saving money in a bank?

- Preferably. Because banking institutions are generally the most reliable, and they pay interest when you keep your savings there.

- Really? Banks pay interest to people for keeping their money?

- Well, yes, they do. They charge and pay with interest for lending and saving money respectively. Interest is the whole business of banks, but the interest that the bank charges and pays is a somewhat special interest. And it's special because its compound interest, interest that charges interest. You know what interest rate means; you better tell me this first, you know it's a percentage value?

- I've heard those words, but I don't quite understand what they mean.

- I'm going to help you understand, my dear Eduardo.

- Go ahead Mr. Danglar, I am interested in learning these concepts, one day I will create my own business or company and learning this today will help me, right?

- Yeah. Yeah. That's right, Eduardo.

Mr. Danglar explained to Eduardo what the multiplication table is for, who first made sense of the number one multiplication table. Then he was taught a simple way to understand how the percentages are calculated and in short I will show it to you, dear reader. Pay close attention, please.

If you have any number and multiply it by a peso, then you will have that number converted to pesos. For example you have 5 units of banana that are priced at one peso. (5 x $1.00) when you sell it will become five pesos ($5.00)

The cents are represented as a hundred parts of a peso. So $0.01 is a cent, $0.10 is a dime, $0.99 is ninety-nine cents.

When you want to know the percentage of a quantity, you multiply it by so many cents. For example, forty percent of a hundred pesos, you get it by multiplying 100 pesos by forty cents. 100 x $0.40 = $40.00 pesos. This means that 40 is 40% of 100.

Twenty-five percent of thirty pesos you get by multiplying thirty by twenty-five cents. 30 x $0.25 = $7.50 pesos. It means that twenty-five percent of thirty pesos is seven pesos and fifty cents. This is done successively for any quantity.

Something that is also very important to know is that so much percent represents one amount in another. For example, if you had $30.00 pesos and had to spend $7.50 pesos, what percentage did you spend? And what percentage do you have left? To find out what percentage you have left, it is easily calculated by dividing what you spent by the amount you originally had and multiplying it by 100. This is $7.50 / $30.00 = 0.25, if we multiply 0.25 percent, we will get 25%.

If I want to know what percentage I keep, I divide my remaining value by the amount I had. This is $22.50 / $30.00 = 0.75, then I multiply by one hundred. 0.75 * 100 = 75% It means I have 75% of the 30 pesos I had left or 22.50 is 75% of 30.00.

- There are two types of interest Eduardo, one is simple interest and the other is called compound interest. Pay attention.

- Yes, I hear you.

- If I lent you $100.00 pesos, and charged you 10% for the next ten days, how much would you have to give me?

- Well, I'd give you back your $100.00 pesos and give you the 10% that's for an addition, so I have to give you $110.00 pesos.

- That's right Eduardo, this interest rate is called simple interest. You can calculate it as I taught you before, multiplying the 100 pesos borrowed by one peso plus 10 cents. 100 x ($ 1.10 pesos) which will result in $110.00 pesos. But there is one interest, which is what banks use, which they call compound interest.

By way of illustration, let's say that compound interest is like lending you a lower interest rate every day, but in the end it will add up to much more than simple interest.

To continue using the example above, a representation of 10% compound interest would be almost equivalent to lending you $100.00 pesos plus 1% interest generated each day for 10 days. Then you would have to calculate the borrowed value (100) multiplied 10 times by one cent (0.01). This is the same as saying: 100 (1.01) (1.01) (1.01) (1.01) (1.01) (1.01) (1.01) (1.01) (1.01) (1.01) = 100*(1.1046).

$100 * 1,1046 = $110.46 with compound interest.
$100* 1.10 = $110.00 with simple interest.

This means that in the example above compound interest is 46 cents higher than simple interest. This will result in more resources to pay.

- Remember I told you that banks pay interest if you bring money with you? And they charge interest if you borrow money, too? Well, it turns out that banks charge you higher interest if they lend you money than the interest they pay you when you save money.

- Why are you laughing? Is that good, Mr. Danglar?

- Of course, Eduardo, that's very good. Banks are the main partners of the rich, you can count on them to achieve financial freedom.

- But how? You just told me, Mr. Danglar, that they pay very little and that their loans are very expensive. The only ones who will get rich will undoubtedly be the owners of the banks.

- You must build your capital with work and effort. When you work and produce money you must save enough money so that with the interest the bank pays you can live in dignity. Over time you will learn that there are many projects you can work on and you will be able to acquire a little wealth from the help you get from the bank by borrowing a little capital. If your business is profitable, then with the resources you generate, you will be able to pay the bills or bills, including the bank's money with interest, and then, when you finish paying the money you borrow, as long as you continue to generate resources, all the profit will be yours alone.

- Live on the interest? Whoa! - exclaimed the excited boy - that must be great, Mr. Danglar.

- And indeed it is. This is called living off the rent, but you must work very hard to make it happen. You must be disciplined and not out of focus with your plans and goals. If you do that, you'll see how rich you'll be one day.

- What do you recommend, Mr. Danglar?

- The first thing to do is to educate yourself and read a lot so that you have good ideas. Always think about how to do business, identifying the resources that are easy for you to produce or obtain and that may interest others. After you are producing those resources, you must then save; for that you need to always know how much you cost, how many resources you produce and how much resources you have left to enjoy, then sacrifice a little bit of the delights and save to take advantage of opportunities and generate more resources.

- Okay, nice!

- To save is advisable to make use of financial instruments that pay high interest, These instruments are found in commercial banking, but you should only use them when you have built a financial support savings, an amount of resources that you should always have available in case there is an emergency or an opportunity.

- A support is like a little saving, right?

- That's right. That's it.

- How many resources should I allocate to this support?

- It is a good idea to use the support so much that you can use it to acquire the resources you need for several months, without having to work or occupy your time. This will allow you to be calm and relaxed. You will thus be able to take advantage of opportunities and, if it is required, solve the emergencies that arise without going to the usurer lenders. Sometimes it is necessary that we go to the banks for a loan; but keep in mind that this need will only be justified when the resources acquired with the loan will be used for the production of more resources and that these will be enough to pay the bank fees and also generate profits.

- What does usurer mean?

- Lets put it this way, for a loan whose interest would be charged by the bank in a year, with the loan shark that loan would be charged in just one month or 15 days. But you also have to pay back the capital. ''This Danglar said, staring into the boy's eyes as he exalted himself'', that is a usurer.

- That's stealing," said the boy, "that can't be, it's too abusive.
- It is, but people go to the loan shark of their own free will. And the reason they do it is ignorance, that's why I want to get you out of it Eduardo.

- I promise you I will never go to the loan sharks, Mr. Danglar. And if I take out a loan from the bank, it will be to negotiate and produce more money.

- I believe you, my dear boy. I believe you.

- So, when are you going to tell me? I still don't know exactly what financial freedom is.

- That's right, I'll tell you. Financial freedom is the ability to produce the resources you need to live in dignity, without having to employ yourself, without having to use your time on anything but breathing.

- Now I understand, that's why the banks are the main allies.

- That's right. When you've saved a lot of money, you can live off the capital income. That is, the interest they pay you for using the resources that belong to you. When the time comes when your income not only allows you to live in dignity, but also allows you to save, then you have achieved financial freedom.

- Just like you, Mr. Danglar?

- I haven't reached her yet, my dear Eduardo, but I will reach her soon.

- But you don't work and live in dignity.

- it's true, my income gives me a decent living, but I'm very fair and I still can't save enough, if inflation soars soon I'll have to find something to do to generate more income.

- Hahn... ah, I get it. Now I understand.

- A long time ago I retired when I was still young, I had worked a lot and did good business; I saved enough money so that my capital in the banks could produce the resources I consume every day of every month, but I neglected a little and for a few months in a row I forgot how much I cost and started to spend more resources than I had available. I spent for a year the resources that were earmarked for savings, so I couldn't compensate for inflation and I couldn't fight it.

When I realized I thought about it and decided to invest some of my capital in some business with other people, thank God I have not been in trouble, but I thought about it and I realized that these investments are riskier than banks and even though they pay more interest I don't want to use them anymore. I am an old man, I have to make more reliable and low-risk investments in order not to lose my comfort level, so I am making the necessary adjustments to earn a little less money, but without any or with very low risk.

- You're a great person, you're a really rich person.

- You can become one too. You're young, just remember the things I've told you and work hard to be ready when the opportunities come into your life.

- I will do so.

- Do you remember the advice we talked about?

- I remember some of them.

- Tell me to see what you've learned.

- Not to get into debt, know how much I cost, learn how to live on revenues, and I don't remember anymore.

- I will remind it to you, young man. Try to know at all times how much you cost, what and how many resources you need daily during the month and secure them. Optimize the use of the resources you have available, spend only what you require to ensure that your needs are covered throughout the month. Always try to know how much resources you produce, which are easier for you to generate and which of them are also valuable to others, this will allow you to trade and save more surplus resources. Save as much as you can with a purpose and a plan, build financial support to help you take advantage of opportunities or solve future emergencies that may arise. Enjoy the resources you produce without neglecting the other things I've told you before, spending or consuming only the part you have left, so you won't need to borrow or visit the loan sharks. Educate yourself, read a lot so that you always come up with good ideas, always try to think about how to do business, buy at the best price and get the best profit. When you have enough resources, live on the income alone, if you do, you can have all the time available to do what you like and want. -Danglar continued- "Many years ago, a talented engineer from a Caribbean island told me this truth, written by Victor Hugo: 'It is not the machines that drive and drag the world, but the ideas. "I'll add this one for you to combine and make your own judgment. The difference between rich and poor is that there are those who always know how to make money and do it permanently, while the others, on the other hand, although they produce resources, permanently spend them.

So that was the end of Mr. Danglars conversation with Eduardo. It is shown to you so that you can be alert to information that exists and without which you cannot build wealth.

Dear Young Man or woman I invite you to take advantage of your talents, to paint, to sing, to dance, to build, to design computer programs, to make sculptures, to sell, to write, to do everything you can and to try to do it in the best possible way. Sell your talents and try to produce great resources while having fun. If you take out a loan, make sure it is one that pays its own fee and leaves some profit to you.

Also keep in mind that what guides the world are the ideas and these can be produced by everyone, but it is essential to cultivate with the help of reading a critical mind that makes good use of logic and contains a willing spirit. You are young, within you is the energy to change the world, the best of all ideas can be born into you.

www.ingramcontent.com/pod-product-compliance
Lightning Source LLC
Chambersburg PA
CBHW032311240526
45464CB00023BA/2992